Let's Discover The States

Territories and Possessions

PUERTO RICO • U.S. VIRGIN ISLANDS • GUAM
AMERICAN SAMOA • WAKE, MIDWAY, AND OTHER ISLANDS
MICRONESIA

By
Thomas G. Aylesworth
Virginia L. Aylesworth

CHELSEA HOUSE PUBLISHERS
New York   Philadelphia

Created and produced by Blackbirch Graphics, Inc.

DESIGN: Richard S. Glassman
PROJECT EDITOR: Bruce S. Glassman
ASSOCIATE EDITOR: Robin Langley Sommer

3 5 7 9 8 6 4 2
Printed in the United States

Library of Congress Cataloging-in-Publication Data

Aylesworth, Thomas G.
  U.S. territories & possessions.

  (Let's discover the states)
  Includes bibliographies and index.
  Summary: Discusses the geographical, historical, and cultural aspects of Guam, Puerto Rico, U.S. Virgin Islands, American Samoa, and the North Mariana Islands. Includes maps, illustrated fact spreads, and other illustrated materials.
  1. United States—Insular possessions—Juvenile literature. 2. United States—Territories and possessions—Juvenile literature. [1. United States—Insular possessions. 2. United States—Territories and possessions]
I. Aylesworth, Virginia L. II. Title. III. Title: US territories and possessions. IV. Title: United States territories and possessions. V. Series: Aylesworth, Thomas G. Let's discover the states.
F970.A95 1988   973'.09'42   87–18303
ISBN 1–55546–567–6
     0-7910-0547-X (pbk.)

CONTENTS

Bright sunshine on the hills surrounding Aguas Buenas
in the Caguas Valley.

Worshippers entering the white doors of the ancient
Church of San José in San Juan.

The stern walls of El Morro Fortress rising from the
coast.

The sound of waves lapping against the boats moored
in the bay at Las Croabas.

Hard-working sugar cane cutters toiling in a dense field
near Fajardo.

Green hills rising around the edge of beautiful Lake
Yauco.

Let's Discover
Puerto Rico

Capital: San Juan

Commonwealth Flag

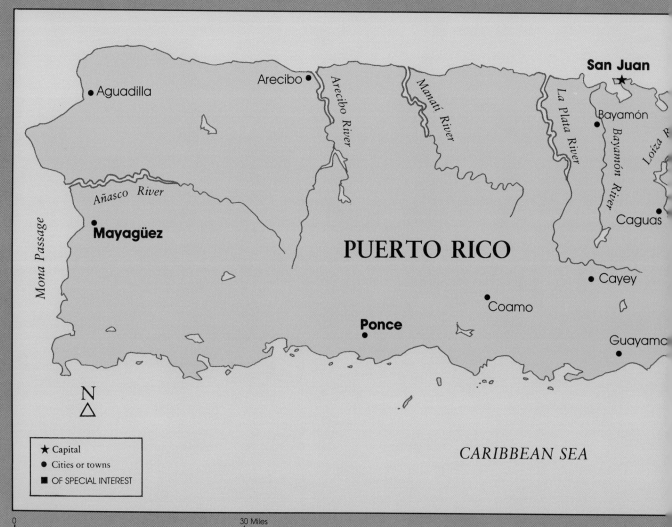

Aguadilla

Arecibo

Arecibo River

Manatí River

La Plata River

San Juan

Bayamón

Bayamón River

Loíza R

Añasco River

Mayagüez

PUERTO RICO

Caguas

Mona Passage

Cayey

Coamo

Ponce

Guayama

N
△

★ Capital
● Cities or towns
■ OF SPECIAL INTEREST

CARIBBEAN SEA

0
30 Miles
0
30 Kilometres

PUERTO RICO
At a Glance

Commonwealth Tree: Ceiba (Silk-cotton tree)

Commonwealth Song: "La Borinqueña"

Commonwealth Flower: Maga

Commonwealth Bird: Reinita

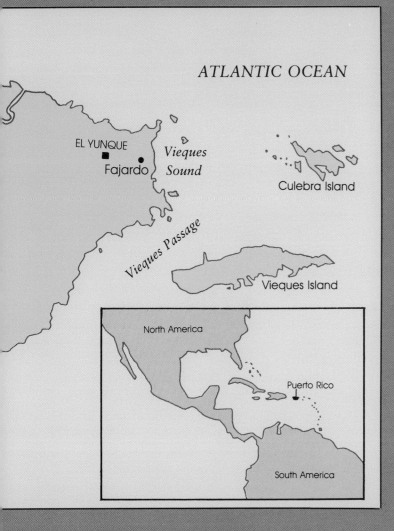

Major Crops: Sugar cane, tobacco, bananas, citrus fruits

Major Industries: Pharmaceuticals, chemicals, machinery

Size: 3,435 square miles

Population: 3,389,686

9

The many beaches and resorts like Guajataca, seen here, have made Puerto Rico a popular tourist attraction. The rugged coast on the north side of the island near Quebradillas is also celebrated for interesting limestone formations.

The Land

The Commonwealth of Puerto Rico (or *Estado Libre Asociado de Puerto Rico*) is a large island between the Atlantic Ocean and the Caribbean Sea just west of the Dominican Republic. The easternmost of the West Indies island group called the Greater Antilles, it is 1,040 miles southeast of Miami, Florida. The commonwealth includes many smaller islands off the coast. Puerto Rico has four main land regions: the Coastal Lowlands, the Coastal Valleys, the Foothills, and the Central Mountains.

The Coastal Lowlands border the island's northern and southern coasts. The northern Coastal Lowlands extend from 8 to 12 miles inland, and their climate is humid. The southern Coastal Lowlands are narrower and drier. These lowlands are the site of Puerto Rico's largest cities, San Juan and Ponce, and most of the commonwealth's industries. Sugar cane is an important crop here.

The Coastal Valleys are found along the east and west coasts. Sugar cane farming is important here, too, and coconuts and fruits are cultivated.

The only one of the 155 National Forests that is tropical, El Yunque (The Anvil), 25 miles from San Juan, covers over 28,000 acres. The rain forest is dominated by two peaks, El Yunque, 3493 feet, and El Toro, 3,526 feet, and is filled with 240 species of trees, countless birds and masses of flowers, including tuberoses, impatiens, and white ginger. El Yunque is also the home of the *coqui,* the tiny tree frog, whose night song resembles that of the nightingale.

The Foothills rise in both the north and the south, extending inland from the Coastal Lowlands. This hilly area has jagged peaks and round basins formed by water that eroded the limestone beneath the hills, causing the ground to sink.

The Central Mountains run east and west in the south-central part of the island. The main range here is called the Cordillera Central; another range, the Sierra de Luquillo, extends off to the northeast. In the Cordillera Central is the highest point in Puerto Rico—Cerro de Punta, 4,389 feet above sea level. The main crop in the western part of the mountains is coffee, and citrus fruits are also grown here. In the east, the most important crop is tobacco.

The coastline of the commonwealth measures some 311 miles. But if the coastlines of the small bays and inlets are included, the total is 700 miles. Along the coast are many beautiful sheltered beaches and harbors.

Local fruits, like mango, melons, grapefruit and papaya can be bought at market stands in the towns and cities across the island. Other street stands serve *pastelillos*, fried turnovers stuffed with meat or cheese; *chicharron*, pork cracklings; or *bacalito*, fried cod batter.

The nearby island of Vieques, a short ferry ride from Fajardo, on the east coast of Puerto Rico, offers secluded beaches of dazzling white sand.

The Arecibo is Puerto Rico's longest river, but none of the island's rivers is navigable by large boats. Their importance is as a source of water for hydroelectric power, industry, and irrigation.

The average all-year-round temperature is a delightful 76 degrees Fahrenheit in the coastal sections, although it is cooler in the mountains. There is only about a 6-degree F. difference between winter and summer. It is moderately humid during the summer months, but not uncomfortably so. Puerto Rico can claim almost perpetual sunshine: it has only about five cloudy days per year. Rainfall varies with location from about 40 to 150 inches annually, with 200 inches falling in the Caribbean National Forest at El Yunque Mountain. There are brief rain showers throughout the year, slightly more frequent between May and December.

Many farmers in the rugged hills still plow with a yoke of oxen. The main crops of the island are bananas, tobacco, sugar cane and citrus fruits.

The History

The Spanish explorer Juan Ponce de Leon established the first settlement on the island in 1508 and served as the governor. A local Taino Indian legend sent him in search of the fabled Fountain of Youth, and he discovered the Florida peninsula. His tomb is now in the Cathedral of San Juan.

Christopher Columbus discovered Puerto Rico on November 19, 1493, during his second voyage to the New World. He called it San Juan Bautista in honor of St. John the Baptist, as reflected in the commonwealth motto from the New Testament, "John Is His Name." Columbus landed on the northwest coast at a spot that is now Aguadilla. He claimed the island for Spain, but made no attempt at colonization.

The first colonizers were Spanish explorers led by Juan Ponce de León, who founded Caparra near San Juan Harbor, in 1508. Located between the present Santurce and Bayamón Districts, it was the second city in the New World. Later, for reasons of defense, the settlement was moved to present-day "Old San Juan" on an island in the bay. Upon arriving, Ponce de León reportedly exclaimed, "¡Qué puerto rico! (What a rich port!)," thus naming the area around the harbor. During the course of the island's history, the names of the capital and the island were transposed: Puerto Rico came to be used as the name of the island and San Juan as that of its capital. In 1514 the island was divided into two districts, each with its own administrator. The eastern section was referred to as Puerto Rico and the western section as San Germán.

After the Spanish settlement was established, the island's Arawak Indians tried to drive out the colonists, but they were attacked ruthlessly. Those who were not enslaved by the Spanish were killed, or succumbed to European diseases to which they had no immunity. By the mid-1500s, few Indians remained on the island that they had called Boriquen.

The settlers from Spain faced many difficulties, including frequent hurricanes, outbreaks of disease, and attacks by the Carib Indians, who lived on neighboring islands. British, French, and Dutch raiders plundered the island, and pirates were a constant threat. But the

The arcaded galleries of the courtyard of the Dominican Convent in San Juan are a fine example of Spanish colonial architecture. Built by the Dominican Friars in the 16th century, the convent has been restored and is used as a library and concert hall. Another wing houses the Pablo Casals Museum.

Depicted in an engraving dated 1860, the residents of San Juan stroll along the battlements of Fort San Cristobal. The forts of Puerto Rico were built to guard the treasure fleets from Spanish America.

Spanish population continued to grow, and forts and towns were built. Sugar cane was introduced in 1515, and slaves were imported from Africa three years later to work on the plantations.

Puerto Ricans began to demand greater independence from Spain during the 1850s, long after the great Spanish Empire of the 1500s was only a memory. In 1897 Spain did grant more local autonomy, and a new Puerto Rican government was set up shortly before the Spanish-American War broke out in 1898. U.S. troops landed on the south coast at Guánica, and Spanish troops retreated before them. The U.S. Navy bombarded San Juan, and the Puerto Ricans refused to cooperate with the Spanish army and navy; instead, they welcomed the American troops. On October 18, 1898, the island was surrendered, and Spain ceded Puerto Rico to the United States in the Treaty of Paris on December 10, 1898. The island remained under a U.S. military government for the next year and a half.

The American occupation meant that the use of U.S. money and postage on the island was official. In April 1900, Congress passed the Foraker Act, which instituted civil government. The arrangement did not please the Puerto Ricans, despite U.S. construction of dams, hospitals, roads, and schools. The Puerto Rican economy depended upon agriculture, and the people resented the fact that U.S. companies were skimming off much of the profit they made from their interests in local plantations and sugar mills.

The Jones Act of 1917 effected a great improvement. It made Puerto Rico a territory of the United States and granted U.S. citizenship to all who wanted it: only 288 people chose not to accept citizenship. Many Puerto Rican men served in the armed forces during World War I, still more during World War II.

Old San Juan, the oldest part of the city, has been lovingly restored and preserved, mixing small businesses with museums, and markets with old houses.

The most familiar landmark in Puerto Rico is El Morro, the great fortress built by the Spanish between 1540 and 1586. It has never been taken from the sea, although the English besieged it successfully in 1598. The Spanish won it back and improved the fortifications. Completed in 1783, it still guards the harbor of San Juan. The tracks for moving cannon to cover the widest field of fire created a pattern of arcs along the walls as seen above.

Rum, made from local sugar cane, distilled and bottled on the island, is one of the most popular local drinks. Puerto Rican rum is also exported all over the world.

One of the most impressive chapters in Puerto Rican history began in the early 1940s. It was "Operation Bootstrap," aimed at economic development that would make the island self-sufficient and raise its standard of living. Puerto Ricans and the U.S. government joined forces for the project. Large farms were broken up, and land was redistributed among farmers. Many old slum buildings were torn down and new housing went up. The educational system was overhauled.

The program was highly successful. New businesses produced chemical and pharmaceutical products, machinery, apparel, and other goods. By 1956 manufacturing had surpassed agriculture as the island's principal source of income, and it has remained in the lead ever since. Tourism has also become a major industry.

It was not until 1946 that Puerto Rico had its first native-born governor. He was Jesús Toribio Piñero, who was appointed by President Harry S. Truman. One year later, the island was given the right to elect its own governor; the first was Luis Muñoz Marín, who took office in 1948.

The Ponce Museum, designed by Edward Durrell Stone, houses a remarkable collection of Old Masters, including works by Rubens, Velázquez and Van Dyck. The Museum also contains many paintings by island and other Latin American artists.

On July 3, 1950, Puerto Rico was granted the right to draw up its own constitution, which was modeled on that of the United States. On July 25, 1952, Puerto Rico became a self-governing commonwealth. During the Korean War, the U.S. Army's 65th Infantry Regiment, made up of Puerto Ricans, won fame for its courage in battle.

Today Puerto Rico is still in a period of rapid industrial growth. Despite the increase in industry, the unemployment rate remains high, partly because of the island's high population density—987 people per square mile. Many Puerto Ricans have emigrated to the mainland in search of new opportunities. Puerto Ricans value their

The streets of San Juan are overhung with balconies, shading the doorways of the shops selling souvenirs, including *santos,* wooden carvings of the saints, as well as ceramics, baskets and *papier mache.*

Arecibo Ionospheric Observatory, on the north side of the island, monitors changes in the layers of the earth's atmosphere.

Hispanic heritage, and the commonwealth offers many cultural facilities, including San Juan's Fine Arts Center and Puerto Rican Family Museum.

When Puerto Rico became a territory of the United States in 1898, only about 20 percent of its people could read or write. With the help of the federal government, public schools were established all over the island and the literacy rate improved dramatically. The University of Puerto Rico, founded in 1903, has its main campus at Rio Piedras and maintains a botanical garden and a Museum of Anthropology, Art, and History.

The three-day fiesta of Santiago Apostal (St. James the Apostle), held in Loisa Aldea every July, combines the island's Spanish Catholic heritage with that of the African slaves who settled the town.

The People

More than 66 percent of Puerto Rico's people live in towns and cities, including San Juan, Ponce, and Mayaguez. More than 99 percent of them are of Hispanic descent, with a small number of Portuguese, Italians, French, and North Americans represented in the population. Some 80 percent of the people are Roman Catholics. Other denominations include the Assemblies of God, Baptists, Methodists, and Presbyterians.

One of the island's great political figures was Luis Muñoz Marín, who was not only the first elected governor, but a driving force behind "Operation Bootstrap" and commonwealth status for Puerto Rico. He was born in San Juan.

In the field of entertainment, prominent Portoriqueños include singer José Feliciano (Lares) and actors José Ferrer (Santurce), Rita Moreno (Humacao), and Raul Julia (San Juan). One of sports history's great baseball players, Hall of Fame member Roberto Clemente, was born in Carolina.

Above:
Roberto Clemente, the popular outfielder for the Pittsburgh Pirates, who won the National League batting championship four times, also directed Puerto Rican efforts to aid earthquake victims in Nicaragua. Clemente was killed in the crash of a plane carrying supplies to Nicaragua.

Left:
Actor/director Jose Ferrer intended to be an architect, but a summer in the theater turned him to acting. He has played such classic roles as Iago in *Othello,* but is best known for his work in the movies. He won an Oscar for Best Actor for *Cyrano de Bergerac* (1950). His other films include *Moulin Rouge* (1953), *The Caine Mutiny* (1954) and *I Accuse* (1957) in which he played Dreyfus.

A street corner in Old San Juan

IN SAN JUAN: *Old San Juan*

The original part of this historic city is filled with tree-shaded streets, old Spanish gas lamps, and 17th-century houses and public buildings.

NEAR FAJARDO: *El Yunque*

"The Anvil" is a towering peak that supports a tropical rain forest filled with brightly colored parrots and wild orchids. It is part of the Caribbean National Forest.

IN SAN GERMÁN: *Cathedral de Porta Coeli*

This "Gate of Heaven Church," with its thick walls and massive doors, is one of the oldest churches in the western hemisphere and maintains an excellent Museum of Religious Art.

AT LA PARGUERA: *Phosphorescent Bay*

On moonless nights one can see the flashing of millions of tiny phosphorescent plants and animals in the water of this bay.

IN SAN JUAN: *El Morro*

This imposing Spanish fortress, built between 1539 and 1787, was used to guard the Bay of San Juan from marauding pirates and foreign invaders.

For more information write:
CHAMBER OF COMMERCE
100 TETUÁN
P.O. BOX S-3789
SAN JUAN, PUERTO RICO 00904

FURTHER READING

Colorado, Antonio J. *The First Book of Puerto Rico*, 2nd ed. Franklin Watts, 1972.

McKown, Robin. *The Image of Puerto Rico: Its History and Its People, On the Island—On the Mainland*. McGraw-Hill, 1973.

Perl, Lila. *Puerto Rico: Island Between Two Worlds*. William Morrow, 1979.

Singer, Julia. *We All Come from Someplace: Children of Puerto Rico*. Atheneum, 1976.

Steiner, Stanley. *The Islands: The Worlds of the Puerto Ricans*. Harper & Row, 1974.

The scenic ruins of Princess Plantation on St. Croix.
Intricate scrollwork on the lacy balconies of
    Government House in Charlotte Amalie.
Fishermen hanging up their nets to dry after a day's
    catch of red snapper.
Cutters wielding their machetes with precision in a
    dense field of sugar cane.
Old stone buildings and pastel-colored houses under
    the summer sun in Christiansted.
Ships rocking peacefully at anchor on Coral Bay, off
    St. John.

Let's Discover

U.S. Virgin

Islands

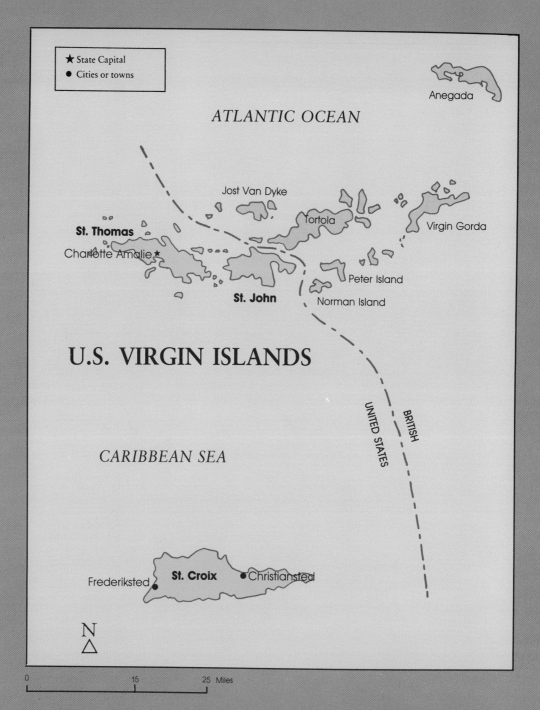

THE U.S. VIRGIN ISLANDS
At a Glance

Flag

Major Industries: Tourism, rum, textiles, pharmaceuticals
Major Crops: Vegetables, sugar cane, nuts

Flower: Yellow Elder or Yellow Cedar
Bird: Yellow Breast
Song: "Virgin Islands March"

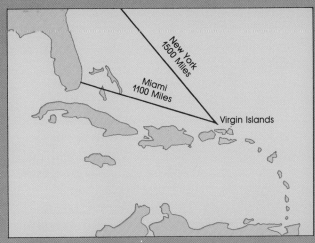

Size: 133 square miles
Population: 101,500

Capital: Charlotte Amalie, St. Thomas

The Land

The U.S. Virgin Islands are about 40 miles east of Puerto Rico, along the Anegada Passage between the Atlantic Ocean and the Caribbean Sea. They include the islands of St. Croix, St. John, and St. Thomas, and many nearby islets. Together with the nearby British Virgin Islands, the group forms the westernmost part of a great chain of West Indian islands called the Lesser Antilles.

The U.S. Virgin Islands are volcanic in origin, and, except for St. Croix, they have rugged, hilly surfaces. Hills on the three major islands can reach heights of 1,500 feet above sea level. Tropical flowers and trees flourish, contributing to the islands' scenic beauty.

St. Croix, the largest of the Virgin Islands, covers 84 square miles and has almost half the islands' total population. St. John has an area of about 20 square miles, three-quarters of which comprises part of the Virgin Islands National Park. St. Thomas covers 28 square miles, and contains the highest point on the islands—Crown Mountain—at 1,556 feet. The remaining islands are too small to be inhabited.

With temperature ranges between 70 and 90 degrees Fahrenheit all year round, the U.S. Virgin Islands have a congenial climate. Trade winds moderate heat and humidity and rainfall averages 45 inches yearly, with the heaviest rains occurring in spring and fall. However, the islands frequently experience a water shortage because of increases in both population and tourism. By law, each house must have its own cistern to catch rain water, the size of the cistern based upon the area of the roof. There are seawater distillation plants on St. Thomas and St. Croix, but fresh water has to be imported from Puerto Rico during droughts.

Magen's Bay, on the Atlantic side of the island of St. Thomas, has clear water surrounded by over a mile of white sand, and remarkable tropical plants among the palm groves. It is considered one of the most beautiful beaches in the world.

Christopher Columbus, a Genovese sailor, is traditionally credited with the discovery of the New World. He did have the idea to sail west to reach to Spice Islands, and convinced King Ferdinand and Queen Isabella of Spain to sponsor a voyage. His small fleet of three ships left Spain on August 3, 1492, and made a landfall at San Salvador, which Columbus believed to be part of Japan, on October 12. He made three subsequent voyages and discovered Puerto Rico, Jamaica and Trinidad. A contemporary wrote that "as a seaman, he had no equal in his generation." The voyages of Columbus drew the American continents into the mainstream of history, while the riches of the new lands gave impetus to the rise of capitalism by adding to the depleted stock of European precious metals, and the balance of political and economic power shifted from the Mediterranean to the Atlantic coast.

History and People

Christopher Columbus named the Virgin Islands and claimed them for Spain on his second voyage to the New World, in 1493. The islands were inhabited by the cannibalistic Carib Indians, who had a small battle with Columbus's crew at Sugar Bay, on St. Croix. The Indians repelled all visitors to their islands until the mid-1500s, when Emperor Charles V of Spain ordered his soldiers to kill them and seize their lands. Those who were not annihilated left the islands before they were taken over by the British and the Danes, who began settling there in the 1600s.

The British came to the Virgin Islands in 1607 on their way to set up the colony of Jamestown, Virginia. At the time, the Spaniards were using the islands' harbors to hide their treasure ships from pirates, but they never settled there. The first European settlers arrived in 1625, when Dutch and British colonists landed on St. Croix. They were driven out in the mid-1600s by Spaniards from Puerto Rico. Twenty years later, the French expelled the Spanish. The French controlled St. Croix until 1733, when they sold it to Denmark for $150,000.

The sugar mill under restoration at Whim Great House, one of the rich sugar plantations built on St. Croix during the 1790s. The sugar economy collapsed in the 19th century following a drop in sugar prices, restrictive import taxes and the emancipation of the slaves in 1848.

Fort Christansvaern on St. Croix was built of brick brought from Denmark as ballast. Completed in 1749, it is a prime example of Danish colonial military architecture and the best preserved of the five forts on the island. The Danish garrisoned the fort until 1878 when it became a courthouse and police station.

The walls of the buildings along Alexander Hamilton Alley in Christiansted were built three feet thick to keep the interior rooms cool. Hamilton, though born on the nearby island of Nevis, grew up on St. Croix, and worked as a clerk in a counting house in Christiansted.

The Danes had claimed St. Thomas by founding a settlement there in 1666, but the colony failed. A successful settlement was made in 1672, and the Danes finally settled on St. John in 1717, when the St. Thomas colony was well established. The Danish West India Company controlled the region's development for a hundred years. Slaves were imported to work on sugar-cane and cotton plantations, and St. Thomas was designated a duty-free port to enhance its commercial importance. Slave uprisings beginning in 1733, the year that Denmark purchased St. Croix, finally resulted in the abolition of slavery in 1848.

The Danish West Indies surrendered to the British twice during the Napoleonic Wars of the early 19th century. During these periods of occupation, so many English-speaking soldiers and sailors were quartered on the islands that English became the common language of the people.

From 1672 onward, the British controlled the rest of the Virgin Islands, separated from the Danish holdings by a channel called the Narrows. These 32 small islands, of which the largest are Anegada, Jost van Dyke, Tortola, and Virgin Gorda, are still a territory of Great Britain.

The Annaberg Ruins on the island of St. John, are a vast plantation complex being restored to show tourists all the steps of sugar production, from the crushing of the cane by the mill, powered by sails to the boiling which removed the impurities. The raw sugar might be treated further to become rum.

Coral World Marine Park on St. Thomas features a multi-level underwater observatory where visitors can see sharks, barracuda and brightly colored tropical fish, including moray eels, among the elaborate coral formations.

Denmark's attempts to develop the Virgin Islands during the latter part of the 19th century were largely unsuccessful, and in 1917 they were sold to the United States for $25,000,000. This purchase provided the United States with a base from which to safeguard the Panama Canal, which had been completed in 1914.

The people of the U.S. Virgin Islands were made citizens of the United States in 1927. After World War II, the federal government set aside some $10,000,000 to improve the islands' schools, hospitals, roads, and sewage and water systems. A new legislature was created in 1955, and three years later the islands' first native-born governor, John D. Merwin, was elected. The College of the Virgin Islands was established in 1962, and the territory now has 33 public elementary and high schools.

About 25 percent of the people in the U.S. Virgin Islands live in the cities of Charlotte Amalie, Christiansted, and Frederiksted. Some 63 percent were born in the islands and 12 percent in Puerto Rico. Other residents come from various parts of the West Indies and North America. The largest religious groups are the Episcopalians, Lutherans, Methodists, Moravians, and Roman Catholics.

OF SPECIAL INTEREST

Tropical fish swim among exotic underwater plants.

ON ST. CROIX: *Christiansted, the Old Town*
This has been called the loveliest old town in the West Indies, with its weathered stone buildings, pastel-colored houses, and charming waterfront.

ON ST. CROIX: *Frederiksted, Fort Frederik*
Built in 1760 by the Danes, the fort has been restored and now contains a museum.

ON AND AROUND ST. JOHN: *Virgin Islands National Park*
The underwater portion of this beautiful park has coral reefs teeming with colorful sea life; on St. John are white sand beaches and forested peaks and valleys.

OFF ST. JOHN: *Coral Bay*
This is one of the best harbors of refuge in the Antilles and was used as a Danish port in the 1700s.

ON ST. THOMAS: *Charlotte Amalie*
The capital city's harbor can accommodate even the largest ships, and its hotels and resorts host visitors to the islands' scenic tropical beaches, shops, and restaurants.

For more information write:
ST. THOMAS AND ST. JOHN: CHAMBER OF COMMERCE
P.O. BOX 324
ST. THOMAS, VIRGIN ISLANDS 00802
ST. CROIX: CHAMBER OF COMMERCE
17 CHURCH STREET
CHRISTIANSTED, ST. CROIX, VIRGIN ISLANDS 00820

Let's Discover GUAM

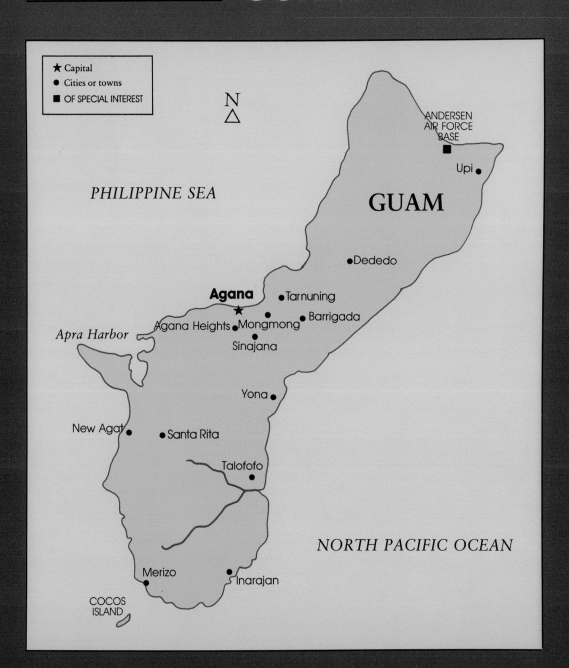

Capital ★
Cities or towns ●
OF SPECIAL INTEREST ■

N
△

PHILIPPINE SEA

GUAM

ANDERSEN
AIR FORCE
BASE ■

Upi ●

● Dededo

Agana
★
● Tarnuning
Agana Heights ● ● Mongmong ● Barrigada
● Sinajana

Apra Harbor

Yona ●

New Agat ● ● Santa Rita

Talofofo ●

NORTH PACIFIC OCEAN

Merizo ●

Inarajan ●

COCOS
ISLAND

GUAM
At a Glance

Flag

Capital: Agana

Flower: Puti Tai Nobio (Bougainvillea)

Bird: Toto (Fruit Dove)

Tree: Ifit (Intsiabijuga)

Nickname: Where America's Day Begins

Song: "Stand Ye Guamanians"

Major Industries: Tourism, textiles, foods, petroleum refining

Major Crops: Cabbages, cucumbers, tomatoes, coconuts, yams

Size: 209 square miles

Population: 110,800

Hikers pause to admire the view from the lower slopes of Mount Lamlam over Cetti Bay on the western side of Guam.

The Land

Guam is the largest and southernmost of the Mariana Islands of the West Pacific. The islands of this region are referred to collectively as Micronesia. Guam is some 1,500 miles west of the Philippine Islands and 3,700 miles west of Hawaii.

Guam's 78-mile coastline is fringed with coral reefs. The northern half of the island is a coralline limestone plateau that was originally covered by thick forests. Many of these forests have been cleared for farms and airfields. The southern half of Guam has low mountains of volcanic origin, the steepest of which is Mount Lamlam, 1,334 feet above sea level.

The island has warm weather year-round, with temperatures ranging from 72 to 88 degrees Fahrenheit. Strong seasonal winds called typhoons sometimes hit Guam with destructive force, and rainfall averages 90 inches per year. The island is also subject to occasional earthquakes.

History and People

Portuguese explorer Ferdinand Magellan, serving the court of Spain, discovered Guam and the islands around it in 1521. He called them *Islas de los Ladrones* (the Islands of Thieves), because the people there helped themselves to goods from his ship after supplying him with food and water. The islands were colonized by Spanish missionaries in 1668, and renamed the Marianas in honor of Maria Anna, the queen of Spain. In 1899, after losing the Spanish-American War, Spain ceded Guam to the United States and sold the rest of the Marianas to Germany. In 1919 Japan obtained a League of Nations mandate over the German Marianas.

Ferdinand Magellan, the Portuguese explorer commanded the first expedition to sail around the world. After finding the difficult passage, now known as the Strait of Magellan, around Cape Horn, he became the first European known to have crossed the Pacific, discovering many of the small islands of Polynesia. Although Magellan was killed by natives in the Philippines, one of his ships, commanded by Juan Sebastian del Cano, returned to Portugal three years after the expedition began.

Residents of Guam, an ethnic mix of Pacific peoples, including Indonesians, Filipinos, Koreans, Japanese and Micronesians, enjoy a feast of native dishes – baked bananas, breadfruit and taro, combined with specialties brought to the islands from the rest of the Pacific.

Japan attacked Guam on December 7, 1941—the same day it launched the surprise attack on Pearl Harbor, Hawaii, that brought the United States into World War II. The island was captured five days later and was not recovered by U.S. troops until July 21, 1944. The U.S. Navy established its Pacific headquarters there the following year.

On August 1, 1950, Guam was declared a territory by the United States, and supervision of the island was transferred from the navy to the Department of the Interior. Its people became United States citizens and elected a local one-house legislature. Beginning in 1970

Guamanians elected their own governor, who had formerly been appointed by the president of the United States. The University of Guam was founded in 1952, and the island has 27 public elementary schools and 9 high schools.

Only about 25 percent of the people of Guam live in cities like Agana and Tamuning. Many of them are native Guamanians, called chamorros—people of Indonesian descent, with a mixture of Filipino and Spanish blood. They speak both English—the official language—and the native Chamorro. Other residents are descended from American, Italian, French, British, Japanese, Chinese, Filipino, and Mexican settlers. About 40 percent of the people on Guam are U.S. military personnel and their dependents. Some 95 percent of native Guamanians are Roman Catholic.

OF SPECIAL INTEREST

AT ANDERSEN AIR FORCE BASE: *Chapel*
This modern house of worship is one of many buildings constructed at the base during the 1950s for U.S. military personnel.

OFF THE COAST: *Coral Reefs and Beaches*
These beautiful reefs, formed by the shells of innumerable tiny organisms, are home to colorful tropical fish and a wide variety of other sea creatures. The white, sandy beaches provide opportunities for swimming, sunning, and water sports.

IN MERIZO: *Water Festival*
Designed for fun, this annual mid-August celebration is a highlight of the year.

NEAR YONA: *Mount Alutom*
This 1,125-foot peak offers a scenic vantage point from which to view the island.

AMERICAN SAMOA

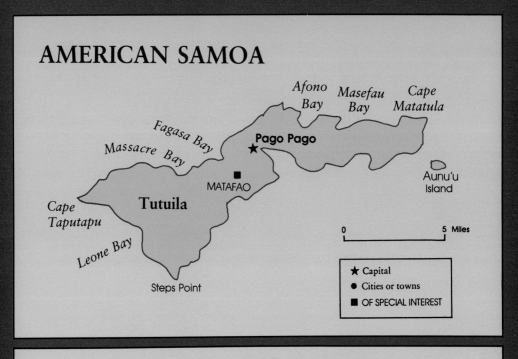

AMERICAN SAMOA

Afono Bay
Masefau Bay
Cape Matatula

Fagasa Bay

Massacre Bay

★ **Pago Pago**

■ MATAFAO

Aunu'u Island

Cape Taputapu

Tutuila

Leone Bay

Steps Point

0   5 Miles

★ Capital
● Cities or towns
■ OF SPECIAL INTEREST

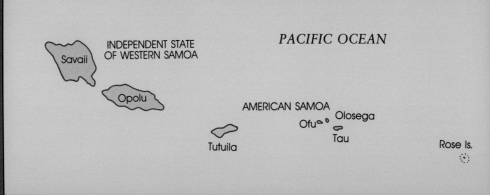

INDEPENDENT STATE OF WESTERN SAMOA

PACIFIC OCEAN

Savaii

Opolu

AMERICAN SAMOA

Ofu   Olosega
Tau

Tutuila

Rose Is.

AMERICAN SAMOA
At a Glance

Flag

Major Industries: Agriculture, handicrafts

Major Crops: Breadfruit, yams, coconuts, pineapples, bananas

Flower: Paogo (Ula-Fala)

Plant: Ava

Motto: *Samoa Muamua Le Atua* (In Samoa, God Is First)

Song: "Amerika Samoa"

Capital: Pago Pago, Island of Tutuila

Size: 77 square miles

Population: 33,800

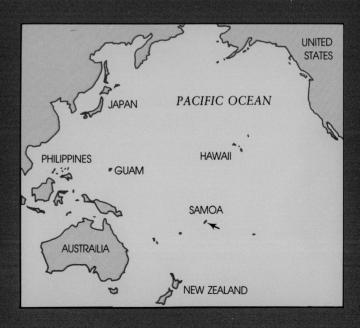

On the largest island of Tutuila, a group of Samoans, who share the charm, gaiety and dignity of all Polynesians, enjoy a cricket match.

The Land

American Samoa is an unincorporated territory consisting of six small South Pacific islands of the Samoan group, some 4,800 miles southwest of San Francisco. They include Tutuila, Aunu'u, Ta'u, Olosega, Ofu, and Rose. Swain's Island, 210 miles to the northwest, is also administered by the U.S. as part of American Samoa.

Tutuila and Aunu'u have an area of 53 square miles. Ta'u covers 17 square miles, and the islets of Ofu and Olosega, 5 square miles. Swain's Island is about 2 miles square.

Some 70 percent of American Samoa is bush, growing on the slopes of volcanic mountains. Coral reefs surround most of the islands, which have a delightful South Seas climate. The principal export is copra (dried coconut), followed by fish products and handicrafts. Tropical fruits, taro, yams, and citrus crops are cultivated. The only wild animals in Samoa are rats, snakes, and birds. The islands are subject to strong hurricanes and gales between January and March.

History and People

American Samoa became U.S. territory by a treaty with Great Britain and Germany in 1899. Local Polynesian chiefs ceded their claims to the islands in 1900 and 1904. Prior to this, the U.S. Navy had used the harbor at Pago Pago as a fueling station, and American Samoa's first administrators were naval officers who ran the islands as a military installation. The welfare of the Samoan people was neglected, except by a handful of missionaries.

In 1951 U.S. president Harry S. Truman transferred responsibility for American Samoa to the Department of the Interior. Since then, the development of the islands has progressed rapidly. Schools have been built, roads paved, housing expanded, and a new jet airport constructed. Because of the islands' spectacular scenery and congenial climate, tourism is a growing industry. In 1978 the first popularly elected Samoan governor and lieutenant governor were inaugurated. Previously, the Secretary of the Interior had appointed the governor. American Samoa has a two-house legislature and an elected delegate to Congress in Washington, D.C.

Most American Samoans are of Polynesian origin, and the largest percentage are Christians. Population is concentrated on the larger islands of Tutuila, Aunu'u, and Ta'u.

A few thousand people live on the islets of Ofu and Olosega, and tiny Swain's Island has only about 100 inhabitants.

American influence is obvious in the menu offered to a customer on Tutuila. The native food includes breadfruit, fresh fish and pork, as well as coconut, which may be also used as a flavoring.

OF SPECIAL INTEREST

AT PAGO PAGO: *Pago Pago Harbor*
This scenic deep-water harbor is the only usable seaport in American Samoa.

IN PAGO PAGO: *The Dry Goods Store*
This store was formerly a hotel where the British author Somerset Maugham wrote his classic short story "Miss Thompson," set in the South Pacific. It was successfully dramatized by John Colton and Clemence Randolph as *Rain*.

NEAR MATAFAO: *Samoan Mountains*
These lustrous violet-tinged mountains rise to their highest point at 2,141 feet above sea level.

WAKE, MIDWAY, AND OTHER ISLANDS

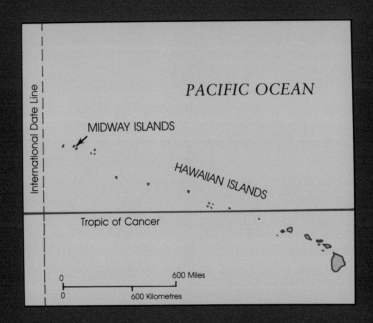

WAKE, MIDWAY, AND OTHER ISLANDS

At a Glance

Size: Wake, Wilkes, and Peale Islands—3 square miles
Midway Islands—2 square miles
Johnston Atoll—1 square mile
Palmyra—4 square miles

Population: Wake, Wilkes, and Peale Islands—1,600
Midway Islands—2,200

Surrounded by a coral reef, the Midway Islands, site of a U.S. naval station, gave their name to the famous World War II battle. The U.S. victory at Midway prevented the Japanese from gaining a foothold from which they could launch further attacks against Hawaii.

The Land

Wake Island, and its sister islands, Wilkes and Peale, form an atoll (low coral reef) in the west-central Pacific Ocean on the direct route from Hawaii to Hong Kong, some 2,300 miles west of Hawaii. There is no fresh water on these small coral islands, and the scant vegetation consists mainly of shrubs and bushes.

The Midway Islands, Sand and Eastern, are located in the North Pacific, about 1,500 miles northwest of Hawaii. They, too, are coral islands.

Other Pacific islands under U.S. jurisdiction include Johnston Atoll (southwest of Hawaii), Kingman Reef (south of Hawaii), Palmyra (south of Hawaii), and the uninhabited Howland, Jarvis, and Baker Islands (southwest of Hawaii).

History and People

Wake, Wilkes, and Peale Islands provide a stopping place for ships and airplanes crossing the Pacific. Wake was probably sighted by the Spanish when they explored the Pacific in the 1500s. The first people to land there were the men of the British schooner *Prince William Henry* in 1796.

Wake was explored and surveyed in 1841 by Commander Charles Wilkes of the United States Exploring Expedition, whose naturalist, Titian Peale, investigated the plants and animals there. The group found no indication that the atoll had ever been inhabited.

The United States claimed Wake in 1898 for use on the cable route between San Francisco and Manila. In 1935 it became a base for air traffic crossing the Pacific. When the United States entered World War II in 1941, Wake became a national defense area. A force of 400 U.S. Marines and about 1,000 civilians held off a Japanese invasion for two weeks, but the islands were finally captured. The Japanese remained there until the war ended in 1945. Since 1972 Wake has been administered by the U.S. Air Force.

The two Midway Islands, Sand and Eastern, were discovered by the United States in 1859 and annexed in 1867. A cable relay station was built there in 1903, and an airport in 1935. One of the most important naval battles in the Pacific theater of operations during World War II was the Battle of Midway, which lasted from June 4 to June 6, 1942. This was the first decisive U.S. victory against the Japanese, and it prevented their occupation of Midway as a base from which they could have attacked Hawaii and other Pacific military installations. The Midways are administered by the U.S. Navy Department.

Johnston Atoll is administered by the Nuclear Defense Agency of the Nuclear Regulatory Commission, and Kingman Reef is under U.S. Navy control. Although there are no residents on Howland, Jarvis, and Baker Islands, the Department of the Interior has jurisdiction over them and over the island of Palmyra, which is privately owned.

Wake has a population of 1,600 and Midway, 2,200, primarily U.S. military personnel.

Let's Discover

MICRONESIA

MICRONESIA
At a Glance

Flag

Size: 716 square miles

Population: 120,400

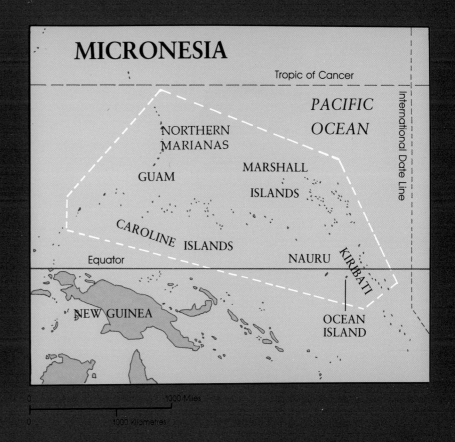

Major Industries: Fish products, copra, handicrafts

Major Crops: Coconuts, breadfruit, melons, tomatoes

Bird Island lies off the northern coast of Saipan, the main island in the Mariana chain.

The Land

Micronesia is the common name for what is officially the United States Trust Territory of the Pacific Islands. It includes three major archipelagoes, or groups of small islands, scattered over 3 million square miles of the Pacific. These systems are the Caroline, Marshall, and Mariana Islands. (Although Guam is part of the Marianas, it is not included in the Trust Territory, since it has its own legislature and governor.)

The Caroline Islands are just north of the equator, between the Marshall Islands and the Philippines. There are more than 930 islands in this archipelago, many of them volcanic, with luxuriant vegetation; others are barren coral islands. Fish products, copra (dried coconut) handicrafts, and vegetables are exported from the larger islands, the best known of which are the World War II Japanese strongholds of Belau, Peleliu, Truk, and Yap.

The Marshall Islands are some 2,200 miles southwest of Hawaii. The 34 small islands in this archipelago are primarily coral. The people of the Marshalls cultivate palm and breadfruit trees, and their livelihood depends mainly on copra and fish. The climate is tropical, but ocean breezes cool the air. Rainfall is light in the northern islands, and heavy further south. The best known of the Marshall Islands are Bikini and Enewetak Atolls, where the United States conducted nuclear tests after World War II, and Kwajalein, the site of a wartime battle.

The 15 Mariana Islands are volcanic in origin, part of a submerged mountain chain that extends 1,565 miles from Guam almost to Japan. The 10 northern Marianas are primarily rugged, some of them with active volcanoes that erupt from time to time. The five southerly islands, which are older than the others, have no active volcanoes. Manganese and phosphate are mined in the Marianas, and farmers produce copra and food crops. The group's most important islands, apart from Guam, are Pagan, Agrihan, Anatahan, Rota, Saipan, and Tinian.

History and People

In 1527 Spain claimed the Carolines, which it sold to Germany in 1899, after the Spanish-American War. During World War I, Japan took control of all Micronesia, including the Carolines, and the League of Nations awarded the Japanese a mandate over the islands after the war. During World War II, U.S. forces captured some of the islands, including Peleliu, after heavy fighting. Japan surrendered in 1945, and the United Nations made the United States trustee of the Carolines as part of the Trust Territory of the Pacific Islands.

The first European to visit what became known as the Marshall Islands was probably a Spanish navigator, Alvaro de Saavedra, who

A young Saipanese girl husks coconuts to sell them to Japanese tourists. Many Japanese visit Saipan for the tropical beaches and pleasant climate.

For many years, the United States carried out hydrogen and atomic bomb testing near the atolls of Bikini and Enwetak. The native Micronesians were removed to other islands, but recently 55 natives pressured the U. S. government to return home.

A monument honors those Korean troops, fighting with the Japanese, who died defending Saipan in June, 1944.

sailed the central Pacific in 1529. In 1788 John Marshall, an English sea captain, explored the islands that were named for him. In 1866 Germany gained control of the Marshalls, which it bought from Spain in 1899. After World War I, they passed to Japanese control through the League of Nations mandate. In 1933 Japan left the League of Nations, sealed off the Marshalls to Europeans, and built military bases on some of the islands as part of the expansionist policy that brought the Japanese Empire into World War II. The United States captured Enewetak and Kwajalein in 1944 and ultimately took control of all the Marshall Islands.

Ferdinand Magellan, a Portuguese navigator in the service of Spain, discovered what are now the Marianas in 1521. Spanish missionaries arrived in 1668, and Spain governed the islands until the Spanish-American War of 1898, after which it sold all the Marianas except Guam to Germany. The Japanese took control of the islands during World War I and held them until 1944, when U.S. forces defeated them in the World War II battles for Guam, Saipan, and Tinian. In 1947 all the Mariana Islands except Guam became part of the U.S. Trust Territory of the Pacific Islands. The Northern Marianas, as they are called, are currently seeking U.S. commonwealth status.

The people of the Trust Territory are primarily Micronesians, whose ancestry includes Melanesian, Polynesian, and Malaysian stock. Only 98 of the Territory's 2,141 islands are inhabited.

INDEX

Numbers in italics refer to illustrations

Photo Credits/Acknowledgments

Photos on pages 5, 6–7, 10, 13, 17, 19, 25, 26, The Rowland Company; pages 8–8, 11, 12,
14, 15, 20, 22, 23, 24, John Florian; page 16, Library of Congress; page 18, New York Public
Library; pages 20–21, Dave Kleinman; pages 27, (both), 52, 53, 55, 60–61, Wide World;
pages 36, 47, Culver; page 43, Coral World.

Cover photograph courtesy of The Puerto Rican Travel Commission.

The Publisher would like to thank Suzanne Worden of The Rowland Company, Susan
Lomenzo, of Development Counsellors International, and Mary Pope Hutson of the U.S.
Department of the Interior for their gracious assistance in the preparation of this book.